Original title:
Buttons of the Heart

Copyright © 2025 Creative Arts Management OÜ
All rights reserved.

Author: Elias Marchant
ISBN HARDBACK: 978-1-80586-046-4
ISBN PAPERBACK: 978-1-80586-518-6

The Layered Embrace

In a world of fluff and thread,
Where laughter echoes, joy is spread.
We wear our layers, soft and bright,
Each stitch a giggle, pure delight.

With pockets wide, for secrets told,
Embraces warm, never cold.
In patterns bold, we dance around,
Finding joy where love is found.

Stitching Dreams Together

A patchwork mind, with colors neat,
Dreams stitched tight, no chance to cheat.
With every poke and every pull,
Our hopes inflating, bright and full.

In a tapestry of goofy schemes,
We sew our laughter with wild dreams.
Each thread a whim, a winking eye,
Together crafting our silly sky.

Seams of Serenity

In cozy seams, we find our peace,
A funny quilt that will not cease.
With yarns of joy and threads of cheer,
We stitch our moments, year to year.

Beneath the chaos, we find the calm,
A silly patch, a loving balm.
With every knot, our worries flee,
Wrapped up in laughter, just you and me.

Love's Intersections

At street corners, love takes flight,
With silly signs, a comic sight.
We bump and weave, a joyful dance,
In tangled hearts, we take a chance.

With quirky signs and winks of fate,
We navigate this silly state.
In lanes of laughter, we collide,
An intersection where dreams abide.

Love's Tailored Touch

Sewn with laughter, stitched in haste,
Each thread a memory, no time to waste.
Buttons of giggles, on shirts of cheer,
Worn proudly daily, with love sincere.

Tailored moments, oh what a scene,
Fitting together like pancakes and cream.
Life's patterned fabric, colors collide,
In this quirky quilt, we take pride.

Tied Up in Emotion

Twisted and tangled, our hearts entwined,
Like a shoelace knot, where love's designed.
Pull one string, and chaos descends,
Yet through the mess, our laughter extends.

Stuffed in a drawer, emotions abide,
Tugging at hearts, like a playful tide.
With every pull, a giggle or two,
Tied up in feelings, just me and you.

Knots of Compatibility

Tug at my heart, find a snug fit,
As we dance around, never to quit.
Hooks and loops, our playful affair,
In this mismatch, we find a rare flair.

Knotted together, like shoelaces gone wild,
With a wink and a grin, we remain unbiled.
Compatibility's charm, a tangled delight,
In this fabric of life, we shine just right.

The Hook of Hope

With a hook in hand, we cast our dreams,
Reeling in joy, or so it seems.
Hopes dangling lightly, like ornaments bright,
Navigating waters, oh what a sight!

Catch of the day, with laughter we boast,
Baited with humor, we raise a toast.
With every tug, our spirits lift high,
On this fishing line, our love flies by.

Knotted Promises

Twisted threads in a tangled dance,
A promise made in a goofy trance.
With every knot, a snicker flies,
Who knew vows could wear such ties?

Tied to laughter, we trip and spin,
Our quirky fables, where do we begin?
Each loop a giggle, each twist a cheer,
Knotted promises, forever near!

Tapestry of Longing

Stitches of wishes, a fabric bright,
In the loom of dreams, we take flight.
Each thread a story, spun just so,
Tales of longing, in colors aglow.

We sew our hopes with clumsy hands,
Crafting laughter in a patchwork land.
A tapestry woven with playful glee,
Who knew longing could tickle the knee?

Jointed Wishes

Dancing limbs with a wobble and twirl,
Jointed dreams that unfurl.
Each wish a wiggle, a quirky sway,
Making merriment each silly day.

With clickity-clack, we join the fun,
Creating glee when the day is done.
These jointed wishes, what a sight!
Cracked smiles and laughter, pure delight!

The Snap of Companionship

A playful snap, like a clever snap!
Friendships that lend a comical flap.
With every chuckle, a bond takes flight,
Together we shine, both day and night.

Through fits of laughter, we make our way,
With silly snaps that brighten our day.
Companionship's rhythm, a jolly sound,
In laughter's embrace, our joy is found!

The Knots We Tangle

In a drawer, they squirm and twist,
Little loops of fate, not to be missed.
One's a bit loose, another's just tight,
Laughing we fumble, morning to night.

With colors so bright, they misbehave,
Like couples in love, oh so brave!
Tangles and twists, what a mess to see,
Yet somehow, it's all meant to be.

Stitched Together, Apart

We stitch our dreams with thread so fine,
Sometimes we stray, where do we align?
A stitch here, a stitch there, hold on tight,
While laughing at patterns that just feel right.

Unraveled moments, oh what a scene,
Frayed edges remind us of places we've been.
Still, with each loop, we giggle and cheer,
Because patching it up can be quite the career!

Patches of Passion

Old fabric tales, stitched with delight,
A quilt of our quirks, woven up tight.
Each patch tells a tale of laughter and fun,
Though sometimes we fight, we still come undone.

With colors that clash, we muddle through,
In mismatched moments, our love only grew.
It's a riot, a dance, this fabric of fate,
With every oddity, we celebrate!

Heartfelt Attachments

From sassy to classy, they hang out in rows,
Each one a tale that only love knows.
With winks and a nudges, they start a big show,
Who knew we'd collect such a vibrant tableau?

Each clasp holds a secret, a memory dear,
With laughter and joy, they draw us near.
In a world of fast fashion, we stand out in glee,
These ties that bind us are quirky and free!

The Closure of Love

In a world of knots and thread,
I sew my hopes and fears instead.
Quirky cloth and silly seams,
Stitching up my wildest dreams.

Life's a tailor, quite absurd,
Fashioning love, not a single word.
With laughter, I thread this knotted part,
Creating warmth, a nutty art.

Heartfelt Closures

Zippers stuck and buttons lost,
A stitch in time, oh what a cost!
Giggles echo as I mend,
Each little flaw becomes my friend.

Through wobbly seams and clumsy threads,
I forge connections, but not with dread.
In my closet, love's parade,
Sassy shirts and pants bespoke, I'm made.

Emblems of Sentiment

A patchwork quilt of silly thoughts,
Wearing laughter, I've got lots!
With every patch, a quirky tale,
Adventures stitched with love's detail.

In this fabric of delight,
Heartfelt laughter takes its flight.
A whimsy dance, my sewing spree,
Creating joy, just wait and see!

Attachment in Fabric

Mismatched socks, a color clash,
In the fabric world, we make a splash.
Each quirky print, a love anthem,
Stitched together in rhyme and rhythm.

With ribbons tied and flair to spare,
I wear my heart – a stylish wear.
Sewed with laughter, patched with cheer,
My whimsical closet draws you near.

Love's Needlework

In the fabric of affection, I stitch,
My heart in a quilt, a little embellish.
With thread of laughter, I bind us tight,
But where's the seamstress? Oh, what a sight!

Poking my finger while trying to sew,
You'd think by now, I'd surely know!
Each stitch a giggle, every knot a cheer,
This love's a craft, and it's quite sincere!

Diagrams of Devotion

With pins and patterns, we draft our dance,
Scribbled sketches of a charming romance.
But I lost the map, where did it go?
Now I'm sewing circles, just moving slow!

Lines all crooked from the love we share,
You'd think we plotted it with such care!
But each wobbly curve is a joy divine,
In diagrams so silly, our hearts align!

Embraced by Threads

Wrapped in threads of our silly dreams,
Tangled in laughter and playful schemes.
You bring the yarn, I'll fetch the jokes,
Together we weave, oh how it pokes!

A tapestry stitched with a cautious hand,
Snags in the fabric, but oh, how we stand!
Each loop a chuckle, each twist a kiss,
In this woven mess, there's nothing amiss!

Woven Whispers

Whispers of love in stitches and seams,
Crafting a quilt full of wild dreams.
With every jab, we laugh and we play,
Who knew romance would go this way?

In tangled threads, our secrets reside,
A patchwork of joy with you by my side.
So let's keep sewing this grand little tale,
With humor and heart, we will never fail!

Tightly Wound Affections

In a pocket of laughter, I found you,
Stitching joy with threads of bright blue.
You tie my shoelaces into a bow,
While I trip on words I don't even know.

With needles of humor, you poke at my side,
Trying to keep that silliness tied.
Every joke bounces like a rubber band,
In this fabric of life, I can barely stand.

Your quirks are the stitches that hold us in place,
Like a shirt that's two sizes too large for the race.
But we laugh as we waddle, let's dance the charade,
In this patchwork of love, we're perfectly made.

Fastened with Care

I fasten my hopes with the weakest pin,
You laugh as they wobble, not sure we'll win.
With tape and a dream, we stick it all down,
In the circus of love, I'm the clown with a frown.

A car that's all buttons and wonky in turn,
We laugh till we cry, while the engine does burn.
You tighten the screws while I loosen the grip,
In this fastened adventure, let's take a wild trip.

Heartfelt Threading

With each little thread, our quirks intertwine,
Like mismatched socks that look perfectly fine.
You're the needle that pokes at my peaceful seams,
While I wrangle with life, bursting at the beams.

We patch up our laughter, sew stories anew,
Stitching together like an odd couple's glue.
In this fabric of fun, with buttons askew,
Every quirky moment is stitched just for you.

The Sewn-Down Dream

In our quilt of odd moments, we toss and we turn,
With snags in the seams, but we never quite learn.
You thread me with giggles that fray my best plan,
While I knot up my thoughts, like a confused fan.

Here in the chaos, our laughter's the seam,
As we navigate life in this sewn-up dream.
With a twirl and a spin, let's dance to our tune,
In the fabric of funny, we're healed by the swoon.

Closure's Embrace

In a world where zippers sigh,
I button up a tearful eye.
Sewing laughs with every thread,
Stitching smiles where fears have fled.

A clasp of joy, a snap of glee,
Each loop a dance, a jubilee.
With every tug, a hearty chuckle,
A sewn-up heart, a merry buckle.

Patching love with comic flair,
Tangles lead to playful air.
In the fabric, tales unfold,
Quirky yarns that never get old.

Heartstrings in Stitches

Life's a fabric, full of quirks,
With stitches tight and funny perks.
I thread my fears into a seam,
And patch them up with a wild dream.

Each tug brings laughter, little pins,
As snags become our goofy wins.
Unraveled quirks, a vibrant hue,
With every knot, a tale anew.

Laughs and stitches intertwine,
In playful jests, our hearts align.
A needle's wink, a playful jest,
In this tapestry, we find our best.

The Fabric of Connection

Woven threads in a comical dance,
Each fiber tugs at chance's stance.
A patchwork quilt of joy and jest,
Stitched together, we find our zest.

In laughter's shade, we spin and weave,
A tapestry where hearts believe.
With every tug, we pull and tease,
A fabric bond that aims to please.

Jokes embroidered in seams so fine,
Our quirky stitches, a perfect rhyme.
Unraveled tales that make us grin,
In our fabric world, love always wins.

Cherished Fastenings

In the closet of my mind,
Fastenings are sweetly lined.
A quirky pin, a vibrant patch,
Each hold a giggle, none to catch.

With every snap, a grin unfolds,
As laughter leaks from button molds.
Sewing tales where humor's bright,
Our bond, a dress of pure delight.

Tightly stitched with gleeful threads,
A playful quilt where joy spreads.
Together fastened, hearts in glee,
Our playful seams, a jubilee.

Clutching at Love

I found a sock beneath the bed,
It whispered sweet nothings, so I stared.
My cat looked jealous, let out a sigh,
As I told my sock to give love a try.

I tried to hug it, it slipped away,
Decided socks weren't here to stay.
When it comes to love, who needs a match?
A cozy sock's warmth is quite the catch.

But then came a sudden, fuzzy cat,
He cuddled my foot and wore my hat.
In the game of love, who can resist?
The charm of a cat is hard to miss.

So here's to friendships, both warm and bright,
Whether with socks or cats in the night.
I'll keep on clutching what love might send,
In this quirky adventure, my heart will mend.

The Lacing of Longing

A shoelace tangled in a tree,
Rode out the wind, just like me.
I cried for shoes that felt so tight,
And laughed as they danced in the bright sunlight.

Those sneakers waited by the door,
With dreams of running, oh to soar!
But every time I tried to tie,
I made a mess, but still, I'd fly.

The dog thought my struggle was a game,
He barked with glee, not a hint of shame.
With every twist, he brought me cheer,
As I laced my shoes year after year.

In the lacing, I found a twist,
That love can be a shoelace tryst.
So here's to laughter, and falls from grace,
Life's funny dance, what a wild chase!

Closure in Compassion

In the cupboard lay an old sock pair,
One sock was holey, with a serious flair.
The other one laughed, 'Let's go for a ride!'
Together they giggled, like young love's tide.

They jumped into the washing machine,
Spinning and churning, just like a dream.
But when they came out, oh what a sight,
The holey sock wore a grin, pure delight.

'Don't worry,' said the holey one with glee,
'My charm can weave us in harmony.
Who needs perfection, it's all in the fun,
Together forever, let's bask in the sun.'

They danced around the laundry room floor,
Finding closure in laughter, who could ask for more?
Compassion lives where the mismatched play,
In the quirky sewn threads of love every day!

The Intertwining of Souls

Two straws in a milkshake, oh what a thing,
Swirling together, just waiting for spring.
With a mischievous sip, they giggled with glee,
In a frosty delight, finding sweet harmony.

Strawberry whispers and chocolaty sighs,
As they enjoyed their confection with eyes.
"It's the best time to twinkle," they said with a cheer,
"Connecting like hearts, let's make it clear!"

They jostled and danced in a sugary swirl,
Oh, the love that came in a milky whirl.
Their intertwined path felt so very right,
In the froth of their joy, they soared into the night.

So here's to the stories of straws and shakes,
Where laughter and love are the sweetest of cakes.
They spun a tale of souls that unite,
In the fun of the fizz, love ignites!

Bindings of Belonging

In a world of mismatched socks,
Where laughter pairs with silly mocks,
We tie our quirks with thread so bold,
In friendship's fabric, fun unfolds.

A stitch here and a patch right there,
We gather together with love to spare,
Our bonds are sewn with laughter's thread,
In every quirk, our hearts are wed.

With every giggle, every cheer,
We fasten memories crystal clear,
In this tapestry we call our own,
We're snugly stitched, never alone.

So let us dance in styles unique,
With mismatched patterns, quite antique,
For in each laugh and playful jest,
These bindings hold our hearts the best.

Love's Tiny Fasteners

My heart's like a coat with buttons askew,
Fastened tight with giggles, just me and you,
In this crazy closet, all bright and bold,
Our laughter loops, a sight to behold.

With tiny clips and snaps that gleam,
We button up bright hopes, stitch a dream,
Each quirky joke, a playful clasp,
In this silly dance, together we'll clasp.

Oh, what a mess, these fasteners bring,
Yet they hold us close, let our joy take wing,
We wrangle our feelings, no need to fret,
With every chuckle, we're more tightly set.

So let's embrace these playful ties,
In mismatched styles, we'll improvise,
For love is sewn with laughter's thread,
Tiny fasteners, where joy is spread.

The Art of Connection

In a world of snippets, threads, and yarn,
We weave our tales, no cause for harm,
Connections like fibers, some tangled, some free,
In this artsy dance, just you and me.

With playful knots and loops that twist,
We create a patchwork, can't resist,
Each laugh an embroidery, vibrant and bright,
In the art of connection, we take flight.

We gather our moments, from silly to sweet,
Our hearts like laces, a fun little feat,
The ties that we make are never too tight,
In this quirky quilt, everything feels right.

Stitching memories under the sun,
With every connection, another day's fun,
So here's to the threads that hold us dear,
In this wild tapestry, we have no fear.

Fastened Feelings

Oh, the feelings we patch with glee,
Woven together, just you and me,
Like zany hats on a windy day,
Our fastened feelings are here to stay.

With an errant button and threadbare laugh,
We tie up our hopes in a funny craft,
Each quirky snicker, a seam in our hearts,
In this whimsical dance, everyone's parts.

We gather the moments, big or small,
In our fastened feelings, we stand tall,
With every giggle and mischievous grin,
We patch up the rips, let the joy begin.

So here's to the bonds, all mismatched and cute,
In this playful chorus, we sing to our root,
Fastened feelings, a laughter-filled art,
In the patchwork of life, we're never apart.

The Velcro of Connection

In a world of sticky things,
We find our quirks and flings.
Like Velcro we attach,
With laughter as our match.

Sometimes we come apart,
A tugging from the heart.
But once we re-align,
We're laughing in no time.

With every silly fall,
We bounce back through it all.
Adhesive jokes we share,
In moments light as air.

So pull and push with glee,
Let's stick together, you and me!
We're held by bonds so fun,
Connection's just begun!

The Bind of Beliefs

In the fabric of our minds,
Are knots of all kinds.
We tie our thoughts in threads,
And laugh at what life spreads.

A belief can be a leech,
It clings and won't let free.
But when we cut the string,
Oh, what a joy it brings!

We'll argue over tea,
Like it's a grand decree.
But in our playful fight,
We find our urge for light.

So let's embrace the mess,
In our tangled finesse.
With humor we'll amend,
Our nonsense knows no end!

Heartfelt Stitches

Needles of wit we wield,
Sewing laughs on the field.
With threads that intertwine,
Our stories funny, divine.

A stitch here, there, a patch,
In our fabric, we'll attach.
With every quirky seam,
We craft a joyful dream.

Each poke brings out a grin,
Even when we sin.
Unraveled tales we tell,
In our patchwork, all is well.

So gather all your yarn,
In this warmth, we shall charm.
We'll quilt our hearts in glee,
With stitches weaved so free!

The Twine That Holds

In the garden of our days,
Twine connects in crazy ways.
With every twist and twirl,
Our friendship's quite a whirl.

We bind our dreams with glee,
While tangled in a tree.
A knot beneath the sun,
Our laughter has begun.

Through thick and thin we sway,
Like twine that will not fray.
If one of us trips low,
We wobble, then we grow.

So grab the twine, let's play,
With silly games each day.
Together we will hold,
A story to be told!

Tension and Release

I wore my emotions like a hat,
Each feeling tangled—what of that?
When love's a game with rubber bands,
You stretch too far, it slips through hands.

A tug of war with sock and shoe,
Where heartstrings play a game of two.
Why do I miss the simple cues?
Like when you joke, I'll trip on blues.

It's like a dance of twist and shout,
But someone's jammed the door to out.
I laugh so hard, I snort in glee,
Yet still I trip—please set me free!

So here's to love, a quirky ride,
With all its ups and downs, we glide.
Dance like a wobbly chair on legs,
And laugh our hearts out—no more begs.

Interwoven Tales

In the fabric of giggles, entwined,
Are stories of hearts, each one designed.
A fumble here, a laugh out loud,
Mixed threads of love wrapped in a cloud.

A mismatched sock and a sock puppet,
Whispering tales of how hearts strut it.
With playful banter and quips that fly,
We weave our yarn, oh my, oh my!

Like cats on the prowl, we sneak around,
Trying to find that lost love sound.
But chaos reigns in this wild spree,
When puns collide, and we just can't see.

Oh, let's embrace the tangled threads,
With laughter loud and silly spreads.
Our stories spin, and so we dance,
In the tapestry of love's sweet chance.

Heartfelt Closures

Closing time, yet hearts stay ajar,
We laugh at love—it's never bizarre!
With silly faces and winks that shine,
Why does it feel like we're in a line?

A wardrobe full of mismatched clothes,
Reminds us of every flare that glows.
Fridge magnets whisper, saying, 'Stay!'
While socks conspire in their own way.

Heartfelt goodbyes turn into jests,
"Did you bring snacks?" is how love rests.
We hug as though we're made of fluff,
What's a farewell when laughter's tough?

So as we wrap this joyful spree,
Let's close the door with laughter free.
And next time we meet, do wear that hat,
Where hearts can giggle—imagine that!

The Pull of Insignificance

In this vast world, we're specks of dust,
But boy, do we shine—oh yes, we must!
Like ants on a picnic with crumbs galore,
Love's a toast; can we have some more?

With cat socks and pie charts of dreams,
Our joy wears pajamas, or so it seems.
When tiny mishaps make big ol' waves,
We steer our ships through love's silly caves.

What's crucial today may fade by night,
Yet giggles linger, taking to flight.
So let's toast to the moments so small,
For they hold the heart, the biggest of all.

In this grand tale of thrill and jest,
Insignificant? No, we're truly blessed!
With every chuckle and heartfelt flair,
Our simple lives feel beyond compare.

Pieces of Us

There once was a sock, so mismatched,
Adventuring solo, no plans attached.
It danced on the floor, rolled under the chair,
Searching for socks that were simply not there.

With buttons all jiggly, they laughed out loud,
As shirts fluttered proudly, feeling so proud.
The closet a carnival, fabrics in glee,
A T-shirt said, 'Hey, come play with me!'

A clumsy old quilt with patches of fun,
Told tales of the days when it snuggled the sun.
With sleeves in a twist and a collar cocked,
They pranced like fireworks, no one was shocked.

So here's to the zippers and threads somehow frayed,
To life's little wiggles, the laughter displayed.
In the wacky wardrobe, let merriment reign,
For life's a grand mix-up, with joy in the chain.

The Fabric of Yearning

In a dress made of dreams that once came alive,
A patchwork of wishes began to derive.
It tangoed with shirts in a playful attire,
While ties, jiggly-jointed, said, "Dance till you tire!"

A hoot from a hoodie, full of delight,
Said, "Life's too short to miss fun every night!"
With capes that could fly if you tickle them right,
They soared over sofas, oh what a sight!

The yarns tell the stories, such laughter between,
As khakis confide in their sage cousin Jean.
With a belt in the mix, they swayed side to side,
Embracing the chaos of love's boundless ride.

Here's to fabrics, their charm and their cheer,
To the stitches that bond us, year after year.
For sewn in our laughter, our troubles depart,
In the fabric that holds all the threads of the heart.

Threads of Affection

There once was a thread, so silly and bright,
Wrapped round a button, it giggled with fright.
It danced to the rhythm of fabric's sweet song,
Telling the tales where the silly belong.

A zipper with swagger, loved to tease,
While ribbons would shimmy, quite eager to please.
The threads had a meeting, beneath a loud door,
Deciding to mingle and dance on the floor.

With a paperclip pinching its pal's fancy shirt,
A moment of laughter, amidst all the dirt.
"Oh clothes, let's unite in a joyous embrace,
For life's but a party, at a curious pace!"

And so through the rummage, the jests took their flight,
In the closet's wild laughter, day turned into night.
With seams that were howling and patterns that spun,
They stitched up a story, where fun had begun!

Stitches of Emotion

A patch on the elbow just craved for some fun,
While pockets played peek-a-boo, one by one.
They giggled at wrinkled old socks banging toes,
As a pair of suspenders put on quite a show.

A pocket protector, so dapper, so sly,
Watched the playdates of bows like stars in the sky.
With polka dots bouncing and stripes in a whirl,
They twirled through the air, in a fabulous swirl.

The buttons all joined, a quirky parade,
Each stitch woven tightly, no love to evade.
And as seams came together in joyous disarray,
They knew that together they'd conquer the day.

So let's raise a glass to this lively embrace,
In the closet of memories, a colorful space.
With laughter and fibers, our stories entwined,
No fabric can tear what emotions have lined.

An Ensemble of Emotion

In a land where feelings roam,
A quirky quilt of hearts found home.
Each patch a laugh, a joyful snort,
Sewn with care, a jolly sort.

When laughter threads the fabric tight,
And quirks come out in plain sight.
A dance of love, a silly waltz,
Through stitching woes and laughter faults.

Those seams might fray, but don't you fret,
For every chuckle, a perfect set.
A patch might slip, but heart's alive,
With every stitch, we laugh and thrive.

So let's embrace this wild design,
With jolly prints and crazy line.
For in this cloth, we join the fun,
An ensemble woven, just begun.

Fastenings of Fidelity

On a shirt of loyalty, buttons gleam,
Each one a promise, a silly dream.
With mismatched styles and threads askew,
They hold together, me and you.

In the closet of our bizarre attire,
Laughter tailored, never to tire.
From ties that wobble to shoes that squeak,
Each fastening speaks, unique and cheek.

With a zip, a snap, and a great big grin,
Our quirky wardrobe welcomes kin.
For every clasp that breaks and falls,
We'll patch it quick with memories' calls.

So let's embrace our goofy gear,
In this wardrobe, we hold most dear.
Fastenings of love, stitched with glee,
Together forever, just you and me.

Mending Love's Canvas

In a patchwork world we find,
Stitching laughter, love entwined.
A little fray, a lot of fun,
Crafting warmth, we are not done.

With mismatched threads, we weave our fate,
A work of art that's truly great.
We patch the holes with jokes and cheer,
Sewing memories we hold dear.

With needle's point, we take our aim,
Quirky colors play the game.
A canvas bright with silly parts,
Each stitch reveals our funny hearts.

So let us mend with laughter's thread,
Through every tear and joy we've spread.
In this tapestry called love,
We find our wings and rise above.

Gossamer Threads of Sentiment

Woven strands of smiles so light,
In breezy whispers, hearts take flight.
A tickle here, a playful tease,
In every laugh, we find our ease.

Floating dreams on silken string,
Silly secrets that we bring.
Together we dance on threads of air,
With every giggle, a loving flare.

Like fairies flitting through the night,
Connecting us with pure delight.
A net of joy that holds us tight,
Gossamer threads make everything right.

In this tapestry of glee,
We find the magic, you and me.
So let us twirl in life's embrace,
On threads of sentiment, we find our place.

The Unseen Hand That Holds

An invisible force, what a thrill,
Guides our hearts with gentle skill.
With every pull, a laugh escapes,
The hand that jests, our joy shapes.

In moments great, in moments small,
This unseen hand catches our fall.
With silly pranks and a wink of fate,
It ties our souls, oh isn't it great?

In life's wild dance, it leads the way,
Tickling dreams as we sway.
With every chuckle, a knot's secured,
A bond of fun, forever assured.

So let us bow to this guiding hand,
In the circus of life, take a stand.
For in its embrace, we truly see,
The unseen hand that sets us free.

Attaching Joy and Sorrow

With every smile, we clip and bind,
Enhancing moments, love defined.
A playful tug on dreams so bright,
Joy and sorrow twirl in flight.

We dangle hopes like shiny charms,
In the midst of life's sweet calms.
A laugh, a tear—what a blend,
Both sides of love we commend.

Each moment stitched with tender grace,
Joy's embrace and sorrow's trace.
Together woven, the fabric stays,
In tangled threads, we find our ways.

So as we attach both dark and light,
We celebrate each funny sight.
For in this symphony of rhyme,
Joy and sorrow dance through time.

Interlaced Hearts

In a fabric shop, tangled threads,
I lost my way, tripped on some beads.
Stitching laughter, with seamstress grins,
Our quirky love, where the sewing begins.

A needle pierced, with a silly sigh,
We mend the gaps, just you and I.
Your snags and flaws, I love them all,
Like mismatched socks in a wooden stall.

With every tug, a giggle sneaks,
You thread my heart, your laughter speaks.
In colorful yarn, our jests are spun,
And all our stitches, they are such fun!

So let's create, an oddball scene,
With knitted jokes, in colors obscene.
Each row we craft, a wild new start,
In this patchwork love, we'll never part.

A Quilt of Memories

Fabric squares, all shapes and sizes,
Dancing memories, in funny disguises.
Grandma's tales, stitched in a fray,
Laughter and love, sewn every way.

A quilt of dreams, with patches of cheer,
Each cozy corner holds a story dear.
A spilled drink leads to a threadbare laugh,
While chasing cats, we stitch our path.

In mismatched colors, we take our stand,
A patchwork journey, oh so grand.
With every fold, a giggle bursts,
In our quilted life, joy's never cursed.

So let's snuggle close, on this comfy spread,
With silly adventures, in stitches we're fed.
Each knot we tie, with a chuckle in tow,
This quilt of ours, we'll never outgrow.

Latches of Togetherness

Lock and key, they fit just right,
With silly twists, we dance at night.
A quirky latch, a symbol so true,
You're the only one that opens me too.

Our laughter echoes, like rusty hinges,
With every joke, reality cringes.
We create sparks, like latches that cling,
In this whirlwind of love, we laugh and sing.

Tangled up in life's little traps,
Side by side, no room for gaps.
As we turn and twist, in playful glee,
Our hearts entwined, just you and me.

With every click, our secrets unfurl,
In this crazy dance, we give it a whirl.
So let's latch on tight, silly and bold,
In our wacky love story yet to be told.

The Fabric of Us

Woven together, like threads of a loom,
Creating a tapestry that chases the gloom.
Every stitch tells a jest, a game,
In the vibrant life, we're never the same.

With patches of laughter sewn into place,
Each moment we share, we honor with grace.
A reckless seam, that's how we roll,
Stitching our quirks, that's how we console.

Caught in a snare, of fabric and fun,
With every tickle, together we run.
Our hearts like cloth, a cozy embrace,
In this madcap race, we find our space.

So let's weave our dreams, with colors so bright,
In the fabric of us, there's always delight.
Hand in hand, let's craft our art,
Together forever, we'll never part.

Sewing Together Solitude

In a world of threads and seams,
I stitch my hopes with silly dreams.
A needle dances, takes a twirl,
While fabric giggles, gives a swirl.

My lonely thoughts begin to play,
They jump and hop, a quirky ballet.
With scissors sharp, I snip the hush,
Creating chaos in a rush.

Every patch, a secret shared,
In vibrant colors, nothing's spared.
I thread my fears right through the lace,
And laugh at stitches out of place.

So here I am, a seamstress proud,
Crafting smiles amidst the crowd.
With every tug and playful knot,
I find my joy in what I've got.

Affections in Every Loop

Loop and twist, with laughter's thread,
A heart that spins, then jumps ahead.
Embroidered quirks in every fold,
Whimsical stories stitched and told.

A yarn ball bounces, what a sight!
It rolls away, oh what a fright!
With winks and giggles, it returns,
So many lessons, what fun we learns!

Each loop, a hug with gentle squeeze,
Ticklish yarn that's sure to please.
In this patchwork, nothing's trite,
A silly dance beneath the light.

Woven quirks and laughter's call,
I find my warmth in threads so small.
In every stitch, the joy we weave,
In funny patterns, we believe!

The Latch of Dreams

Unlocking hope with whimsical keys,
Each click and clack brings silly glee.
A door that creaks with laughter wide,
    Invites the silly spirits inside.

In corners where the shadows play,
My wild dreams just like to sway.
A latch that grips, then pops real loud,
My heart bursts forth, bright and proud.

With every turn, I find a twist,
A comical world I can't resist.
I gather joy like loose change found,
With trials that tickle, I'm spellbound.

The keys may jingle, dance, and tease,
In this house, I do just as I please.
With laughter locked in every room,
My dreams have space to burst and bloom.

Adornments of Longing

I wear my wishes like a crown,
With jewels made from laughter's sound.
With every charm that dangles free,
A silly echo follows me.

Each bead a story, funny, bright,
They twinkle, sparkle in the light.
With necklaces of quirks I hang,
In every twist, my heart will sang!

Earrings of laughter, oh so bold,
They whisper secrets, never told.
With every chime, they tease and cheer,
Adorning hope, chasing the fear.

So here I prance in silly style,
With trinkets that make all who smile.
In every adornment, joy's intent,
A funny heart, so full, so lent.

Sewn Memories

In a drawer where secrets lie,
Patchwork dreams and laughter fly.
A lost sock found, a tiny cheer,
Stitched together, memories near.

Every thread tells tales of woe,
Sowed with glee, and frolics flow.
Forty quirks become a quilt,
In tangled yarns, new joy is built.

Unexpected colors clash and blend,
Frayed edges where the stories bend.
A seam undone brings giggles loud,
Life's tapestry, a jumbled crowd.

With needle's poke, we dance and weave,
Each stitch a wink that we believe.
Sewn with whimsy, mischief's art,
Our cozy fabric hugs the heart.

Heartstrings Untangled

A yarn ball rolls, chaos ensues,
Giggling knots, the heart's own muse.
Frogs in love, all hopped about,
Ribbons tangled, oh what a rout!

Two socks mismatched; oh, what a pair,
Each one claims it's made with flair.
A quick tickle, a silly dance,
With all this fun, how could romance?

Laughter echoing in the air,
A thread pulled here, a tug pulled there.
A frayed end shows the way we play,
In life's grand fabric, humorous sway.

Unraveled it's fun, when hearts go wild,
Every moment, the inner child.
In tangled strings, our joy's profound,
Where love gets lost, freedom's found.

The Pinch of Passion

With a pinch of thread and a wink,
Crafting delight, before you blink.
A mismatched button stole the show,
Laughter folds in, just like dough.

A silky scarf makes quite the fuss,
As it trips you with playful thrust.
Each hem's a giggle, every seam a smile,
Fashion faux pas that's worth the while.

Oh, the fun of flirty stitches,
Twisting feelings, love bewitches.
With a snip and a swish, we come alive,
In this fabric patch, our hearts thrive.

Stitch by stitch, the dance grows bold,
A tapestry of joy to behold.
The pinch of passion, snuggled tight,
In our crazy craft, we find the light.

Love's Fabrications

A patchwork heart, all colors bright,
Crafted crazes with pure delight.
Wobbly zippers and a quirky bow,
Chasing hiccups, love's comic show.

With crafty scissors and messy glue,
We build our dreams right out of the blue.
Silly shapes in a jolly mess,
Each wild creation, well, it's the best!

Behold the fabric of our fate,
Laughter layers that we create.
With quirky seams, every hug is grand,
In playful creations, hand in hand.

Quirks and quibbles are what we wield,
In love's design, pure joy revealed.
Swapped and stitched, our hearts will twine,
In this fabric fun, our stars align.

The Clasp of Togetherness

In a world of mismatched shoes,
We find love in silly hues.
With giggles shared over burnt toast,
Together we laugh, and that's no boast.

Your socks are always left behind,
Yet somehow, we're perfectly aligned.
In laundry wars, we play our part,
Winning hearts with a silly start.

We dance in puddles, splashing wide,
Stomping through life, side by side.
With pancakes flipped and syrup fights,
Our love's a riot, full of delights.

In a realm of quirky quests,
You're my partner in silly tests.
With each small quirk, I've found my place,
In the clasp of joy, I see your face.

Unraveled Affections

Two threads tangled on the floor,
We laugh as we search for more.
Your hair in my soup, what a find,
Yet still, you're the best kind.

A mix-up of random odds and ends,
We create chaos, but that's what blends.
With every mess, a chuckle grows,
Our love unravels, that's how it goes.

There's magic in clumsiness we share,
Like heavy stepping on a dare.
You trip and fall, I simply grin,
In this wacky dance, we both win.

With every knot, our bond won't fade,
In goofy moments, laughter's laid.
Unraveled threads may look absurd,
But stitched together, they sing like a bird.

Ribbons of Romance

We wrap ourselves in tangled bows,
Where laughter's light, and mischief grows.
With silly hats and goofy cheer,
Our quirky love is crystal clear.

A picnic spread, we take a bite,
You throw a grape; oh what a sight!
With ribbons tied on every snack,
Our tummies ache, but there's no lack.

Jumping in puddles, seeking bliss,
A water fight ends with a kiss.
Our hearts like ribbons, flay and twirl,
In a playful dance, we both whirl.

In paper hearts and colors bright,
Each little mishap feels just right.
With each laugh shared under the sun,
Ribbons entwined, we've only begun.

A Tangle of Heartstrings

In a mess of shoelaces, we collide,
Tripping over love we can't hide.
With every stumble, giggles grow,
A tangle of strings, we steal the show.

Your dance moves make me lose my way,
Spinning 'round like kids at play.
With every twist and silly cheer,
A symphony only we can hear.

You serenade me with off-key notes,
In life's grand jest, we're the best folks.
With paper airplanes soaring high,
Our heartstrings pull, you and I.

In the chaos of smiles and cheer,
I find my rhythm when you're near.
Through tangled laughs, our song rings true,
In this dance of love, it's me and you.

Fasteners of the Soul

In the closet of my feelings, there's a hue,
A collection of fasteners, all askew.
My sock drawer's a realm where chaos has reign,
Amidst tangled ties, who can find love's gain?

One hook's for laughter, another for tears,
Each clip's a memory, stitched through the years.
If only one clasp could hold it all tight,
We'd avoid wardrobe malfunctions at night!

A snap here, a tug there, it's all such a mess,
Yet somehow the jumbles bring warmth, I confess.
With buttons and zippers, I navigate this maze,
Dodging fashion faux pas in hilarious ways!

So laugh at my buttons, my quirky décor,
These fasteners hold stories, and oh, so much more!
When styles clash wildly, we dance in delight,
For love's an odd outfit, fitting just right.

Clasped Emotions

My heart has a latch that won't quite unstick,
Holding onto memories, both silly and thick.
With a clatter of laughter, emotions collide,
A wacky parade where my quirks are my pride.

There's a snap for the giggles; a zip for the sighs,
A buckle for blunders, and oh, how it flies!
If only my feelings could come with a tag,
Saying, 'Be gentle, don't give me a snag!'

Each clasp is a story, some light and quite fun,
Twisted in ribbons, under bright summer sun.
I wrangle the chaos, a mountaineer bold,
With the laughter of mishaps, my heart's never cold.

Through zippers and Velcro, emotions stay tight,
Clasped in absurdity, we share each delight.
In the closet of humor, we fashion our way,
With quirks in our pockets, brightening the day!

Ties That Bind

In the comical world, where laughter is loud,
We tread on connections, we're humorous and proud.
A knot in my shoelace is love's playful bow,
Tying me to chaos, but I'm learning, you know!

With mismatched socks and ties that are bright,
We stumble through life with a wink and a bite.
Friendship's a ribbon that flutters and sways,
Ties that bind us in bonkers, delightful ways!

For every mishap, there's one quirky thread,
That links all our laughter, spinning joy in my head.
Each knot tells a tale, with a giggle or two,
Of the adventures we share, and the craziness, too!

So here's to the ties that hold tight with a grin,
To the slips and the trips that we gracefully spin.
In this zany ensemble of life's endless show,
The bonds made in folly will always just glow.

Sewn Into Our Being

In the fabric of feelings, my memories weave,
Sewn in with threads of what we choose to believe.
Each patch, a delight, a puzzling disguise,
With stitches of giggles and some errant cries.

A hem for the happy, a cuff for the sad,
With patterns of laughter that make my heart glad.
Quilts of connection, so bright and unique,
When I thread through the moments, my joy finds its peak!

Through seams of affection, we quilt life's own craze,
In pockets of whimsy, we gather our days.
With layers of stories, some silly and sweet,
Each patch tells a tale, completing the beat!

So let's cherish our fabric, our stories all sewn,
With stitches of friendship, we're never alone.
For in every odd seam, every thread that we share,
Lies the laughter together, a joyful affair!

Unraveled Affection

In a drawer of dreams, I find,
A mismatched pair, quite unrefined.
One's got flair, the other's shy,
Together they laugh, oh what a pie!

They jingle and jive, in playful schemes,
Stitching together our wacky dreams.
With every tug, a giggle it brings,
A tangled tale of quirky flings.

When the cat jumps up, they scatter about,
Rolling away, oh what a rout!
In a game of chase, they play and spin,
These tiny pals, where love begins.

With every clasp and silly twist,
Happiness weaves through the mist.
In this chaos, there's joy anew,
Our laughter sewn in, just like glue.

The Clasp of Memories

I found a clasp from days of yore,
It squeaked and squirmed as I pulled it more.
A tale untold, in rusty gold,
Of treasured moments, brave and bold.

Each click recalls a time to share,
School days, love notes, and fleeting dare.
A picture formed, with silly grins,
As each story starts, the laughter wins.

In pockets deep, it's held so tight,
Memories play in the soft twilight.
With each embrace, it rays the glow,
Of dorky dances and a funny show.

So raise a toast to those old days,
Where every clasp holds silly ways.
For laughter's thread will never break,
In that clasp of mine, heart's keepsake.

Hidden Fasteners

Beneath the bed, a treasure found,
Small fasteners that make no sound.
They whisper tales, of hugs and sighs,
Invisible threads, connect the ties.

One's a hero, with a golden sheen,
The other shy, wearing faded green.
Together they hold, yet love them both,
In funny dances, no need for oaths.

They cling and cling, what a sight!
Dressed up in mischief, day or night.
With every giggle, they make a show,
Who knew fasteners could steal the glow?

Though hidden away, they spark delight,
With every tug, they shine so bright.
In a world of love, they dare to play,
Our little secret, come what may.

Soft Touch of Love

In the cupboard high, a soft embrace,
A world of fluff, in the quiet space.
Every touch brings a cheerful smile,
A warmth that lingers, more than a mile.

Little fibers twist and twine,
Creating joy as we brightly shine.
Through playful dances, we spin around,
In soft touch, true love is found.

We yarn and weave, in jolly cheer,
Tickling hearts, bringing near and dear.
Each snuggle holds a laugh or two,
Where gentle threads pull me close to you.

So cherish the soft, the smiles we wear,
With each little touch, we bond and share.
In every stitch, love's giggle grows,
In this fabric, our happiness flows.

A Pinprick of Passion

In a drawer of dreams, they lay,
All the buttons lost, gone astray.
I found one that says, 'Let's be bold!'
But it's sewn to a sock, if truth be told.

I tried to stitch a heart to my shirt,
But ended up causing a bit of hurt.
It poked me once, it poked me twice,
Now I just wear it as a fashion slice.

Each button boasts a silly tale,
Like the one who tried to sail.
It hit a wave and made a splash,
Now it's a joke—what an unexpected crash!

So here's to buttons, quirky and grand,
That hold together more than we planned.
They may be mismatched, a ragtag crowd,
But they giggle in my drawer, so loud!

The Closure of Kindness

I stitched a smile on my old backpack,
Hoping it helps when I hear a whack.
A careless shove, there went my lunch,
Now sandwiches mix with buttons—what a crunch!

Each time I zip, I hear a cheer,
From buttons that say, 'We're always near!'
They pop and crackle, it's quite a show,
Filling my heart with buttoned-up glow.

Strangers stare, 'What's that on your bag?'
I just laugh, 'Oh, it's not a drag!'
A fashion faux pas, or a wise old chap?
Let's be honest—it's just a nap!

So here's to closures, clunky and cute,
That hold our stories, each joyous loot.
They're a kick, a chuckle, a happy surprise,
With every zip, a day jubilant flies!

Mixed Threads of Memories

In the attic, a box full of fluff,
I found weird buttons, more than enough.
A purple one giggled, a green one danced,
They whispered tales of just a chance.

"Remember the time you wore me on a coat?
You said I looked like a loveable goat!"
I chuckled at memories, a tape on repeat,
With buttons as witnesses, none of them neat.

There's one that claims to be a star,
But it's shaped like some old, rusted car.
I tried to wear it, felt a bit daft,
Now it just sits, a laugh in the craft.

Yet in each thread, a story is spun,
A wacky parade, where we all become one.
I'll keep them close, these quirky delights,
For every button brings back wild nights!

Twisted Ties of Love

Oh, love's a thread with knots galore,
Some ties are fierce, while others just bore.
I tied my heart with a shoelace once,
Lost my footing, but never my dunce.

In the laundry, a button popped free,
Rolled under the couch, oh, woe is me!
It clinks and clanks like a tiny bell,
Singing sweet tunes of 'we'll never dwell.'

So I'll wear this mismatch with fancy flair,
A collection of chaos, love in the air.
Every twist, every twirl, what a show!
A heart made of buttons with nowhere to go.

So raise a glass to ties that intertwine,
With every misstep, we've made them align.
For love is a patchwork, ruffled and spry,
Like crazy button tales that never say bye!

Threads of Emotion

There once was a shirt in a drawer,
With colors that danced like folklore.
When it heard a good joke, oh so loud,
It laughed till the seams were proud.

A sock chimed in with a pun,
Saying life's a stitch and a run.
Each thread in the fabric would grin,
Ready for chaos to begin.

Worn by a kid with a smile bright,
The outfit was quite a silly sight.
It twirled and it spun, all in fun,
Daring a game with the sun.

So here's to the clothes that we wear,
That share funny tales everywhere.
In laughter and cheer, they unite,
Dancing through days, pure delight.

Fastened Whispers

In a closet of secrets, they play,
A bowtie and jeans, what a display!
The belt told a tale of a feast,
While flip-flops giggled, to say the least.

Lace-up shoes planned a sneaky retreat,
While sandals conspired to create heat.
Whispers of fashion, oh so sly,
Stitched stories together, oh my!

Pockets promised treasures untold,
Like crumbs of snacks and tickets of old.
Each item was zesty, a laugh to ignite,
In the kingdom of fabric, all felt just right.

So fasten your fittings, don't fear the style,
Let laughter emerge, unfold and compile.
With each quirky fit, a new tale to share,
In the realm of attire, we find joy everywhere.

The Ties That Bind Us

A quirky old tie found in a rush,
Dreamed of a party, oh what a crush!
It fancied a dance with a hat so broad,
Beneath the disco ball, how they trod.

Suspenders made jokes that went woefully wrong,
But the audience laughed, joining along.
In this fabric-filled tale of delight,
Together they sparkled, oh what a sight!

The pocket square blushed from the fun,
As the socks paired up, two hearts now one.
Straps and seams formed a merry twirl,
In the wacky world of the fabric swirl.

From old cardigans to vests of cheer,
Each stitch made it clear, love is near.
In the tapestry woven from laughter and light,
The ties that bind us, keep hearts so bright.

Sewn with Secrets

A jacket with pockets deep and wide,
Held secrets of laughter no one could hide.
Each button a witness to tales so grand,
Of mischievous squirrels and gifts unplanned.

The seams stitched giggles through years gone by,
As time flew past like a butterfly.
A zipper whispered stories of rain,
While sleeves flapped around like a wild train.

Each tear in the fabric a sign of fun,
Dancing with dust from the setting sun.
With patches aplenty, the stories grew,
In the quilt of our lives, so warm and true.

So wear your best fabric with joy and glee,
For secrets are treasures, as funny as can be.
In the tapestry woven, we laugh and ignite,
In a world full of whimsy, our hearts take flight.

Connected by Threads

In a world of fabric, we dance and twirl,
Sewing up laughter as we spin and swirl.
Stitching our stories with colorful flair,
Who knew that thread could give such a scare?

When tension mounts and stitches break,
We laugh at the chaos that we make.
Our patchwork antics in the sun's warm glow,
Every loop and knot tells a tale of woe.

With mismatched colors, we patch and mend,
Creating a fabric where laughter won't end.
A tapestry filled with the quirks of our hearts,
Together we thrive, it's where the fun starts.

Through snags and tangles, we bravely survive,
In this fabric of life, oh, how we strive!
As we stitch our lives with a thread so strong,
We find humor woven where we belong.

The Weave of Desire

Oh, the fabric of life, it pulls and it twirls,
As we weave silly dreams, and hope it unfurls.
With needlepoint visions and laughter so bright,
We snip all our worries, and dance into night.

From fabric scraps, our love has emerged,
In wild patterns where joy has converged.
With each clumsy stitch, we surely create,
A quilt full of laughter, we share on our plate.

We tailor our moments, fit snugly like jeans,
A patchwork of fun, sewn right at the seams.
With every slight snafu, we both roll our eyes,
Stitching together our most foolish ties.

So come take a peek at this crafty affair,
As we stitch up the world, with plenty to share.
In a weave of desires, with threads that unite,
We'll laugh at the mess, our hearts feeling light.

Stitched Together

In the fabric shop of dreams and laughter,
We sliced through the tedium, chasing after.
A quirky design with patches galore,
Every stitch that we take opens a door.

The fabric of friendship, quirky and bright,
In patterns of chaos, we giggle with light.
With each silly patch, our hearts grow in size,
We find hidden treasures in laughter and ties.

Though frayed at the edges and wild in the seams,
We craft our own joy, while unraveling dreams.
With whimsy and cheer, we measure our thread,
Creating a kaleidoscope under our bed.

So let's quilt our lives with what makes us smile,
Through stitches and laughter, we'll go the extra mile.
In this grand creation, we both dare to play,
Stitched together forever, come what may.

A Patchwork of Affection

In this patchwork quilt, we gather our dreams,
With scraps of the past, and laughter that beams.
Each piece stitched tightly with whimsy and flair,
Reading our patterns, they show that we care.

Here's a pocket of joy where memories live,
We patch up the moments that laughter can give.
With quirky designs and the colors we choose,
We create our own fabric, refusing to lose.

It's frayed at the edges, but oh, what a whole,
A quilt made of giggles, each one plays a role.
We sew up the laughter, embrace every woe,
In this charming patchwork, our love tends to grow.

So let us assemble this colorful stash,
As we stitch up our lives, we'll have quite the bash!
In a world brought together by needle and thread,
A patchwork of affection that never will shred.

The Fabric of Together

In a patchwork world, we stitch our dreams,
With mismatched colors, overflows of seams.
A quirky quilt of laughs and tears,
We wrap it tight, despite our fears.

A fabric soft like grandma's hugs,
With sticky spills and peanut bugs.
We patch the holes with jokes and cheer,
Creating warmth from what we wear.

The Thread That Connects

A little thread can hold so much,
It binds our hearts with every touch.
Like spaghetti strands in a big bowl,
Twisted up, yet still whole.

With silly knots and tangled lines,
We dance around like goofy signs.
What holds us close is often fun,
Together we shine like a rising sun.

Weaving Through Emotions

Weaving laughter into our day,
With silly patterns that won't fray.
Each stitch a smile, each knot a cheer,
Creating fabric that is dear.

In threads of joy, we quilt our woes,
Knocking out fears as the fun grows.
With playful weaves, we dance and prance,
Life's a fabric woven with chance.

The Knots We Tie

Tying knots with ribbons bright,
Turning moments into pure delight.
In every twist, a giggle hides,
As tangled laughter often abides.

With a wink and a twist, we tie it tight,
Life's a party every night.
In the chaos, we find our way,
Through silly knots, we dance and sway.

www.ingramcontent.com/pod-product-compliance
Lightning Source LLC
Chambersburg PA
CBHW060114230426
43661CB00003B/175